Pursuing a life of glory

James Seager

ISBN 9781723906459

Contents

Introduction

At its' core, the life of glory is about receiving the grace and mercy of God and then demonstrating it to the heavens and the world. If you have faith in Jesus, been forgiven of your sins and brought into the family of the Church, then you have started this life. Your life is a visible statement of God's generosity and compassion to spiritual forces and contemporary culture.

However, people don't reach the height of glory as soon as they come to Christ. God calls us to engage in a journey of moving from glory to glory. Part of that is discovering the specific ways God wants you to demonstrate more of His grace and mercy to the world. The purpose of this book is to help you in that journey. By going through the chapters that follow, you will learn to recognise what God wants you to do during the next season of your life. This will help you to show His glory to your world in increasing measures.

In this book you will discover:

- How God's personal plan for your life fits with His eternal purpose for the Church
- How to create forward momentum in your life of glory
- How God wants to use our past to propel us forward into His plans

- How to discover what God wants you to do in your future
- What you can do in the present to move onto the next step of your life of glory
- What the world would look like if every Christian pursued this life

Throughout this book there are questions that will help you dig further into this subject and apply it to your life. At the end of each chapter is space for you to journal the answers to these questions or other thoughts.

Going through this book with a friend or in a group will help you get even more from this book, as you pursue the life of glory together.

God's great plan for the church

God's grand scheme

God has a plan for the world. Habakkuk 2:14 "For the earth will be filled with the <u>knowledge</u> of the glory of the LORD, as the waters cover the sea." (NIV) His ultimate purpose is that every individual will have a personal experience of His glory. We see that culminating at the end of time. We read in Revelation 21:23 that, when God makes the New Jerusalem the glory of the Lord will illuminate it. At the end, the world will experience the fulness of His glory.

However, His glory already fills the earth. Numbers 14:21 tells us that "surely... the glory of the LORD fills the whole earth" (NIV). An important principle to note here is that, with God, there is only completeness. He never does anything in half-measures. We may look at our world and see many things that are not glorious: war, famine, social breakdown, immorality. Yet God says, 'my glory <u>fills</u> the whole earth'.

So, we see there is a gap between the reality that God's glory already fills the whole world and the experience of humanity. Closing that gap is God's grand scheme for the Church, which includes you.

Questions:

- In what ways do you see the glory of God being made known in the earth?
- What specific things are going on in your life or the world at large which shows that God's glory isn't yet fully known?

Glorious people, not person

In our culture we place a high emphasis on individual achievement, both in the church and wider society. We encourage people to accomplish the most they can – whether that is in terms of finance, influence, leadership or church ministry. We want people to do all that God has called them to do, on a personal basis.

However, the Bible teaches us that God's purpose is primarily worked out through the people-group of Christians, the body of Christ, the Church; not through an individual, no matter how charismatic, anointed or gifted they may be. Notice that in Revelation 1:6 the declaration of glory to Jesus comes after the statement that "He… has made us to be a kingdom and priests". Glory comes out of a culture of togetherness. Together, God uses the Church to bring an increase of the knowledge of His glory to the world.

Questions:

- Why do you think God wants us to declare His glory out of a 'culture of togetherness', rather than just as individuals?
- In what ways is a united expression of God's glory greater than an individual expression?

Therefore, to move forward in God's plan for your personal life, you need to understand this principle: pursuing the life of glory is firstly about taking our place in the glorious purpose of God for the Church. Then, it is about discovering God's personal plan for your life.

Finding what God wants you to do in the next season is highly important; it's the focus of what this book is about. But, as you work through the chapters in this book, remember that God's plan for you will be intertwined with His purpose for the world and the church. We need to appreciate that wider purpose, as it will set the scene for God's individual plan for our lives.

A declaring Church

The New Testament says a lot about the church. There are many aspects of its' purpose and role. But it could be summed up like this: to declare God's wisdom to the heavens and the world.

Ephesians 3:10-11 "His intent was that now, through the church, the manifold wisdom of God should be made known to the rulers and authorities in the heavenly realms, according to his eternal purpose that he accomplished in Christ Jesus our Lord." (NIV)

We are told later in Ephesians that "our struggle is not against flesh and blood, but against the rulers, against the authorities, against the powers of this dark world and against the spiritual forces of evil in the heavenly realms." (Ephesians 3:10, NIV). It is to these spiritual forces that the Church is to make know the 'manifold wisdom' of God. Whilst these forces know of God and recognise His power they continue to rebel, blind people to the truth of God and draw them further into darkness. By continually reminding them of God's great wisdom we are declaring that our God is Lord over all, and that they have already been defeated.

1 Corinthians 2:7-8 "No, we declare God's wisdom, a mystery that has been hidden and that God destined for our glory before time began. None of the rulers of this age understood it, for if they had, they would not have crucified the Lord of glory." (NIV)

History shows us that people do not understand the wisdom of God; they have no knowledge of Him or His purposes. That was clearly demonstrated when they crucified Jesus, the 'Lord of glory'. They continue to be ignorant today and quash the glory of God when it is revealed. By intentionally declaring God's wisdom to the world we are showing contemporary culture that the glory of God cannot and will not be extinguished.

The spiritual forces work tirelessly to keep people from seeing God's wisdom. The culture of the world is trying to push God's wisdom into a hidden corner. Our purpose is to be a light and city that will not be hidden, but that wars against our spiritual enemy and overpowers the wisdom of this world so that people might know the glory of God.

> **Questions:**
>
> - What are the practical ways that the Church, as a body, can declare God's wisdom to the spiritual forces of the heavens?
> - What are the practical ways that the Church, as a body, can declare God's wisdom to the world?

God's wisdom

So, what is this wisdom that we declare, and how does it increase the knowledge of God's glory?

1 Corinthians 1:21-23 "For since in the wisdom of God the world through its wisdom did not know him, God was pleased through the foolishness of what was preached to save those who believe. Jews demand signs and Greeks look for wisdom, but we preach Christ crucified: a stumbling block to Jews and foolishness to Gentiles, but to those whom God has called, both Jews and Greeks, Christ the power of God and the wisdom of God." (NIV)

The wisdom of God is this: through the death of Jesus people might be saved from sin and live in His power. In short, the wisdom of God is the gospel. This goes against any logical wisdom of this world. God punishing Jesus for our sin and then extending His mercy towards us is foolishness. It doesn't make any sense that He would open a way for us to live in His continual presence and flow in His power through sacrificing His own Son. But that is the wisdom we declare.

It is this gospel, this wisdom, which displays the height of God's glory. 2 Corinthians 4:4 "The god of this age has blinded the minds of unbelievers, so that they cannot see the light of the gospel that displays the glory of Christ, who is the image of God." How is it that this gospel displays His glory? Because it reveals His mercy and grace.

In Exodus 34, we read how God told Moses to stand on a mountain and He would show Moses His glory. On the appointed day Moses stood there, and God came past. As God moved He said this: "The LORD, the LORD, the compassionate and gracious God, slow to anger, abounding in love and faithfulness, maintaining love to thousands, and forgiving wickedness, rebellion and sin. Yet he does not leave the guilty unpunished; he punishes the children and their children for the sin of the parents to the third and fourth generation." (NIV) God declared His glory in the context of Him being compassionate, forgiving and just. The gospel is exactly that. God was just in punishing sin, as it was all put on Jesus. He was also compassionate and forgiving as He opened the way for humanity to be free from the guilt and power of their sin. The gospel, which is the wisdom of God, is His greatest display of glory.

Pulling all this together, we see that God's purpose for the church is to be a demonstration of the gospel. As we do that, then we are declaring His wisdom to the spiritual forces of the heavens and the culture of our day. The result is that the glory, the mercy and grace of God, is known throughout the world.

Question:

- Think of some ways that the gospel has made a
  difference in your life. How does this bring glory to
  God?

How does the Church declare the glorious wisdom?

You have already seen that God's purpose is to show His glory to
the world through the Church; through the togetherness of being a
Kingdom of Priests. Reality is that this only happens when the
members of the Church, the Christians, are living individually in a
way that declares His glory.

In Ephesians 1:3-14 we read that God has done things in us that are
for the 'praise of His glorious grace'. The Greek word for 'praise' is
'epainos', which literally means applause; the showing of public
appreciation. In this passage we see three things which God has
done, that publicly show His grace and mercy: adopting us, leading
us and giving us the Holy Spirit.

- Adopted for the 'praise of His glory'. Ephesians 1:5-6a "He
  predestined us for adoption to sonship through Jesus Christ, in
  accordance with his pleasure and will— to the praise of his
  glorious grace." (NIV) He makes us children. As we live in

---

relationship with God, rather than fear of Him, we publicly show that He is a good, loving and compassionate Father.

- Led for the 'praise of His glory'. Ephesians 1:11-12 "In him we were also chosen, having been predestined according to the plan of him who works out everything in conformity with the purpose of his will, in order that we, who were the first to put our hope in Christ, might be for the praise of his glory." (NIV) God has a plan for our lives that brings us into alignment with His eternal purposes. As we follow that plan we publicly declare that God can take us to a place of wholeness, significance and effectiveness.

- Given the Holy Spirit for the 'praise of His glory'. Ephesians 1:13b-14 "When you believed, you were marked in him with a seal, the promised Holy Spirit, who is a deposit guaranteeing our inheritance until the redemption of those who are God's possession—to the praise of his glory." (NIV) God gives us His continual presence and power through the Holy Spirit. When we are full of the Holy Spirit then we publicly show that God never leaves us and gives us all we need to live an abundant life.

God's wants us, as individuals, to publicly show appreciation for the way we have been adopted, led and filled with the Holy Spirit. As we all do that, together, then the Church advances in its' God-given purpose to declare His glory and wisdom to the heavens and the world.

Questions:

- How can you, as an individual, declare and demonstrate that you are:
  - A child of God;
  - Following God's leading;
  - Filled with the Holy Spirit?

Pursuing your place in the purpose of God

To recap so far: God has brought the Church into being for the eternal purpose of showing His glory - His mercy and grace, the wisdom of the gospel, to the world and heavens. As an individual, God is doing a work of glory in you of adoption, leading and filling with the Holy Spirit, so that the Church's declaration of glory may burn brighter. By pursuing a life of glory, we play an ever-increasing part in the eternal purpose of God for the Church. Therefore, your life's purpose is not to earn lots of money, get a great job, have a big house or be a great leader. Your purpose is simply this: to take your place in the Church's purpose of demonstrating the glory of God to the world.

Questions:

- How do you feel about the fact that God's plan for your life is part of His eternal purpose for the Church?
- What can you do, practically, to ensure that you continue to be part of God's purpose for the Church?

In all that, God does have a personal plan for how you will bring Him glory. That may include being a great leader, having lots of influence, raising a good family or flowing in provision. The point of this book is to help you discover and live in God's plan for the next season of your life. You may have been on this journey for many years – God has some new glory for you to declare at this stage of your walk with Jesus. As it says, "We are being transformed into his image with ever-increasing glory." (2 Corinthians 3:18, NIV). You may be starting out – God wants you to begin radiating out His glory.

Be encouraged to pursue this life of glory, a life of living out the grace of the gospel along with the world-wide body of Christians. In whatever way God leads you to do that, keep chasing after this life. Why? Because there's always more glory; there's always more grace, more mercy to experience and demonstrate.

> **Question:**
>
> - What do you hope will happen as your life goes from glory to glory?

Looking forward

In the next chapter we are going to look at the importance of creating forward momentum in our lives, if we want to live a life where the glory of God is revealed more and more in us. We will then think about how we discover and live in God's personal plan for our lives. Finally, we will consider what it would be like if we were all living in God's plan and taking our place in God's purpose for us – shining out His glory.

"God, give me a vision of the glory that you have for me to receive and to show to the world."

From glory to glory

Growing

2 Corinthians 3:7-18 is a powerful passage. It shows that every Christian has a life of glory and can continue growing in it. You may look at your life today and think it is inglorious; there will be things that do not declare or demonstrate the grace and mercy of God. But, if you have responded to the gospel and have put your faith in Jesus, be assured, there is a level of glory in you.

A lie of Satan is that your mistakes remove the glory. No! The glorious life is received through faith not works. It is kept through faith, not works. You may make many mistakes, but if you keep your faith then you continue to demonstrate God's grace and mercy to the world.

As mentioned in the previous chapter, 2 Corinthians 3:18 says that we "are being <u>transformed</u> into his image with ever-increasing glory." (NIV) This shows us that the life of glory is progressive. We don't reach the height the moment we accept Christ as Saviour and Lord. There is always more to the life of glory for us to pursue.

The Greek work for 'being transformed' in 2 Corinthians 3:18 is 'metamorphoo'; where we get the word metamorphism from. The best example is that of a tadpole turning into a frog. It doesn't have to strive, it just grows. As it grows it changes. What you will see in this chapter is that all you need to do to be morphed into ever-increasing glory is to grow to become more like Jesus; and the more you grow to be like Him the more powerful your life will display His grace and mercy.

Questions:

- What in your life already displays the glory of God?
- Do you feel your life is at a 'higher' level of glory now than when you first came to faith in Christ? If so, how?

One of the most important principles you will learn in this book is this: no matter where you are starting from, the next step in a life of glory is simply becoming more like Jesus. As we grow up in Him, our lives naturally become more saturated with God's glory. We then demonstrate His grace and mercy to the world in increasing measures. This is the most natural thing for a Christian.

Stepping into the glory

2 Corinthians 3:9 "If the old way, which brings condemnation, was glorious, how much more glorious is the new way, which makes us right with God!" The 'old way' refers to the Old Testament law. The

law was good, as it provided an opportunity for people to worship and approach God through a religious system of priests and sacrifices. But as no one could keep the whole law, it only brought condemnation – it just showed people that they could never be good enough. The 'new way' is the gospel. As we saw in the last chapter, the gospel displays the mercy and grace of God at its' highest. It is most glorious!

We receive the gospel message through faith. A faith that causes us to turn away from our old, inglorious ways, and trust only in what Jesus did for us on the cross. There, He died so that the justice of God might be fulfilled, and His grace and mercy extended towards us. As we exercise that faith in the gospel we become right with God.

Being right with God means two main things. Firstly, it means that our sins are wiped out – not just forgiven but washed away. God doesn't see you as someone who has been let off; He sees you as someone who has never sinned! But it also means that we become aligned with His purpose. Being righteous is not just about the absence of sin in our lives, it is also about the presence of godliness. As we begin to live in a right way, the way that God wants us to live, we take our place in the plans and purpose that He has for our lives. We then begin to live 'to the praise of His glory', as we saw in the previous chapter.

So, when we have faith in the gospel, we step into to God's grace and mercy. That takes us instantly into an experience of His glory. This is important because if we want to continue growing in this life, then we must continue to keep our focus on the gospel. If we leave our first love, we leave the root of the glorious life. If we side-line the gospel to a past experience or to a one-off 'spiritual encounter' then we cut off the root. The gospel is what brought us into glory and living in the power of the gospel is what keeps us in glory.

Question:

- What does it mean to you to keep your focus on the gospel?

Gazing on the glory

The most dynamic thing that the gospel enables us to do is to "approach God's throne of grace with confidence." (Hebrews 4:16, NIV). We are brought into a life of glory through the gospel, and then the gospel empowers us to stand in the presence of glory. If you think of Bible examples of people who lived a glorious life, you think of Moses, David, Elijah, Daniel, Paul. What all those people had in common is this: they spent time gazing at the glory of God. They lived for His presence. 2 Corinthians 3:18 "And we all, with unveiled face, beholding the glory of the Lord, are being transformed into the same image from one degree of glory to another." (ESV) It is through the 'beholding the glory of the Lord' that we go from glory to glory.

Gazing on Jesus is not like looking at a picture of His face – we don't know what He physically looked like, but we do have an image of Him. John 1:14 tells us that the very image of Jesus is grace and truth. The only real picture we have of Christ is His forgiveness and generosity: He wiped away our sin and given us all things. Therefore, the only way we can see Him is by gazing on His grace and mercy in our lives. As you meditate on the fact that God has not treated you as your sins deserve (mercy) but has given you all things that you don't deserve (grace), it is then that you gaze on the glory.

Questions:

- Describe some of the things that God has given to you.
- How can you ensure your worship (personal and in church) is focussed on the grace and mercy of God?

The journey of transformation

As we gaze on the grace and mercy of Jesus in our lives we are transformed. It's really a simple process. We become what we think like. If I think a lot of negative thoughts I become a negative person.

If I think a lot of hateful thoughts I become a hateful person. If I fix my mind on the grace of God, then I become a more graceful person. If I focus my thoughts on His mercy, I become a more merciful person. The result is simply this: the more I gaze on the glory, the more I experience the glory. Or, the more I gaze on the image of Christ, His grace and mercy, the more I become like Him.

Earlier in this chapter, it was mentioned that transformation from glory to glory is like the process of metamorphosis – where a tadpole turns into a frog. Likewise, we are morphed or transformed as we gaze on the grace and mercy of Jesus. This happens in the context of a journey. The tadpole doesn't suddenly become a frog, it grows into a frog. As you have already seen, you don't suddenly reach the height of glorious living, you grow in glory.

Here's two practical things to note about the journey of pursuing a life of glory:

- It takes time. There are things we can do to move more quickly from one stage to the next, but you can never get around the fact that growing up requires time. So, be patient with yourself (and others). If you're on the journey of glory that's all God wants. You don't have to be there, just getting there.

- It involves changes. Transformation means that things are different at this stage of life than they were, and they will look different in the next season. Pursuing the life of glory requires that the old goes and the new comes. That is not just a one-off experience; that is a continual experience. And note that this means leaving one phase of glory to move onto a new step – leaving what is good in this season to enter into what is more glorious for the next.

The key here is this: keep moving. If we are prepared to take a journey of change over time, then we are morphed into new phases of glory in our lives. If we stay still then we stall, and ultimately that glory fades. What God wants for us is progress not protection. He wants us to gaze on His image of grace and mercy so much that we journey into new spheres of glory. That can be hard. The way you have declared and demonstrated the grace and mercy of God in the past may need to be left behind. But it's also great because we know that in moving on from glory we enter into new glory. So, in this journey, don't mourn what you are leaving but rather rejoice in what is coming. Embrace the change that God is bringing into your life at this time and pursue the next phase.

Questions:

- How patient are you with yourself, when it comes
  to growing in a life of glory?
- Think back to a time when you felt God calling you
  to do something new. Describe how you felt about
  this and what the impact was of moving forward.

Displaying the glory

When we engage in this journey of being morphed from one degree
of glory to the next, on a personal level, it has a very public impact.
This is exactly what God wants for us. Our purpose is not just to
receive His glory but also to demonstrate it; not just to experience
the power of the gospel but also to declare the power of the gospel.
So, pursuing this life is as much about growing our public impact as
it is about growing our personal experience. There are some great
examples in the life of Moses about how the personal life of glory
brings about a public demonstration of God's glory.

- Moses was a canvas on which the presence of God was
  displayed. 2 Corinthians 3:7 "the Israelites could not look
  steadily at the face of Moses because of its glory" (NIV). Moses'
  face shone with the glory, because He had been with God.
  Somehow, God had painted on Him a visible representation of

His presence. It's not God's norm to make our faces literally shine. It has happened, and it does happen, but it is the exception not the rule. (We don't measure how much time someone has been with God in lumens – the way you measure the brightness of a light bulb.) But, somehow there can be a physical representation of His presence on our faces. People should see God when they look at us. What should the see? Mercy and grace. A great question that we can ask ourselves is this: does my face carry a look of grace? The more we travel on this journey from glory to glory the more our faces display something of the giving and forgiving nature of God.

- Moses was a channel that brought the provision of God. In Exodus 16, the Hebrews complained because they had no food. Moses gets before God, hears His voice and then declared to the people "in the morning you will see the glory of the LORD" (Exodus 16:7, NIV). When morning came manna was lying on the ground. It was God's glory, God's provision that came, but Moses was the channel that brought it. As we pursue the life of glory we can see the provision of God released to those around us. That can happen as we tap into the supernatural provision of God. It can happen through a spirit of generosity. We believe in a generous God – that's what grace is all about. As we are transformed through grace we become generous. Then the glory in us has a public impact as we share the provision that God has given to us.

- Moses was a conduit for the power of God. When the Amalekites attacked the Hebrews, Moses went up a mountain and stretched his hands towards heaven. Exodus 17:11 tells us that "As long as Moses held up his hands, the Israelites were winning, but whenever he lowered his hands, the Amalekites were winning." (NIV) What was happening? Moses was releasing the power of heaven into a battle on earth. As we pursue a life of glory then we can release grace and mercy into real-life situations. Broken marriages get restored, suicidal individuals find hope and debt-bound people are freed; all through the power of God's grace and mercy in our lives. By pursuing the glory, you can bring about breakthrough in your sphere of influence.

The journey of transformation into higher degrees of glory will bring about a greater degree of impact on the world. The more you gaze on God's grace and mercy, the more you are transformed into that image of glory, and then you change situations around you.

Questions:

- In what ways have you benefitted from someone else demonstrating the glory of God to you through:
    - Displaying God's presence;
    - Bringing the provision of God; and
    - Flowing in the power of God.
- Have you got any personal experience of how you have helped someone else by demonstrating the glory of God to them? If so, describe.

Creating momentum

There are several things you can do to practically engage in the life of morphing from one degree of glory into the next degree of glory. Here are three:

- Develop your experience of His presence. Ask yourself this: Do I experience more of God's presence today than I did last year? Our experience of His presence will naturally go up and down – depending on our emotions, health and circumstances. But overall, we should be moving towards a deeper experience of God's presence in our lives. And that experience should be focusing on His grace and mercy towards you. In our worship experience it is possible to focus on the atmosphere more than

Jesus Himself. In your time with God, choose to think more and more of what He's done for you.

- Discover God's plan for you at this season of your life. We are all called to demonstrate and declare the glory of God in a unique way. Every person has unique situations, gifts, skills and opportunities. Our purpose of impacting the world by demonstrating His glory is sharpened when we engage in the specific plan that God has for us. Ask yourself this: In what way does God want His glory to impact the world through me? (You will discover more about that as you go through the rest of this book.)

- Determine to be a bill-board for grace and mercy in every human interaction. Relationships are of the highest importance to God. We can only demonstrate the glory of God out of good personal interaction. Have you ever tried helping someone you've been nasty to? It just doesn't work! By increasing the quality of our relationships with each other we open up greater ways to demonstrate God's mercy and grace to others.

Through developing a life of presence, moving in the plans of God and growing relationships we can bring momentum and acceleration in our journey from glory to glory.

> **Question:**
>
> - In what ways do you want God's glory to be shown in the next year through your life?

Looking forward

In the next three chapters we will explore more about how you can discover the specific ways that God wants you to declare His glory in your life. This will include thinking about your past experiences; recognising the plan of God for your future; and how your decisions in the present can propel you towards the future life of glory. Then we will finish with a vision of what the world would be like if every Christian was living-out the glory of God.

"God, help me to see more of your glory that I might be transformed from glory to glory and show more of your glory to the world."

The past is a springboard into the future

The glory of the past

In Numbers 33 we read that God instructed Moses to write down all the stages of the Hebrew's journey through the wilderness. Some of the locations recorded in that passage were places of power, provision and presence – Sinai where the presence of God filled the mountain, Marah where the bitter waters became sweet, Rephidim where they defeated their enemies. There were also places that are associated with seasons of rebellion, sin and disunity. And God told Moses to record it all – the good, the bad and the ugly. It wasn't to be forgotten but remembered. Why? Because their past reminded them of this: God had led them every step of the way. Through His grace and mercy, He had taken them from Egypt to the border of Canaan. He had not destroyed them, even though He felt like it! Instead He cared, provided and sent His presence to guide them.

As we've been seeing in this book, the life of glory is fundamentally about experiencing, then declaring and demonstrating God's grace and mercy to the world. As Moses wrote Numbers 33, he was telling future generations about that glory – the way that God's grace and mercy had kept them.

God wants you to remember your past. The very fact that you have got this far on your journey declares to you, and the world, that God's grace and mercy is active in your life. Whilst we must never be bound by our history, reminding ourselves of it can release a fresh declaration of God's glory in our lives.

Your past may contain some very inglorious seasons. There may be things you have done that have not demonstrated the glory of God. There may be things that have happened to you, which were beyond your control, that do not demonstrate God's glory: seasons of grief, pain and suffering that were outside your ability to prevent. Your past may also contain some very glorious seasons of success in your family, career or ministry. God's grace and mercy has kept you through the good times and bad – His presence has led you by still waters and through dark valleys. He saved you through the power of the gospel, and He's kept you by that same power. Whatever your story is, it is a story of glorious grace, that has brought you to this place. The glory of your past is not related to whether it has been good or bad, the glory of your past is simply that His grace has kept you until today.

Questions:

- How do you feel about the statement: the very fact that you have got this far on your journey declares to you, and the world, that God's glorious grace is active in your life?
- Are there any specific stories from your history that you could share with others to declare God's glory?

Embracing, not forgetting the journey

The aim of this chapter is to help you to understand that God wants to use all your past experiences to propel you into you next season of glory. We see this very clearly in Romans 8:28-30, where God tells us that, no matter what we've gone through, He causes it all to work together for good.

Romans 8:28-30 "And we know that in all things God works for the good of those who love him, who have been called according to his purpose. For those God foreknew he also predestined to be conformed to the image of his Son, that he might be the firstborn among many brothers and sisters. And those he predestined, he also called; those he called, he also justified; those he justified, he also glorified." (NIV)

God foreknew us. Before our lives began God knew that we would come to faith in Jesus. And, because God foreknew this, He chose us to take a journey of being conformed to the image of His Son, that we might be justified and glorified. The life of glory, of being transformed by the gospel, of becoming more like Jesus, started at the beginning of our lives. Therefore, as we have said, everything that we have gone through is part of that journey.

The result of your mixed history of experiences is your life today. Your life in the present is a product of your past. Your personality and ability, now, are a result of how you have learned to navigate life and respond to events. Your past has shaped you. In whatever way that has happened know this: your history has brought you to this place in your journey, and from here you are able to step into a future glory. The experiences you have been through set you up for the next season.

People sometimes talk about 'putting their past behind them'. That has the tone of forgetting what has happened, brushing it off or getting over bad experiences. Whilst it is always important to move on from our past (that's what journeying is all about) there is huge wisdom in remembering it, as you have already seen. Why? Because God wants to use the lessons and the experiences of our past to equip us in taking another step in our unique journey from glory to glory. As we take time to remember, meditate and learn from our past we find ourselves in a much better place to move into the future.

Your past is not your destiny – God doesn't want you to live there. Your future is not dependant on your past. Instead, God wants to use everything you have been through to be a springboard into a future where you grow in glory! He can pull all those good times and bad times together in such a way that you have a great starting point for your next step. Every past experience, positive and negative, joins together to create a person who can move into a new season in the life of glory that God has called them to. In this way God causes everything to work together for good – all things from our past come together to propel us into our next step.

Question:

- Do you believe that God has really caused all things to work together for your good, in bringing you to this place in your life? Why or why not?
- How does your past give you strength and confidence to continue pursuing the life of glory?

Pulling our history into the present

The story of Joseph, in the Bible, is sometimes considered to be a great 'rags to riches' story. But it's not really a 'rags to riches' story;

it's really a 'glory to glory' story. Joseph started in a place of prominence. He was the favourite son of one of the most socially powerful families of his day. He was part of the chosen people of God, who carried His promise. But, in Genesis 41, we see that his history led him to a place where he stood before Pharaoh as a prisoner with no rights, no power and no authority. He might have felt his life was completely inglorious. Yet this was where the grace of God had brought him to.

Right there, as he stood in the throne room, he had three choices: does he wallow in self-pity, rekindle the arrogance that took him down the path to slavery in the first place or pull all his learning and experience together to step into a higher level of glory? He chose the latter. Right there, in the throne room, Joseph chose to embrace everything from his past to propel him forward. There are three elements from his past, in particular, that enabled him to take that step.

- His lessons in humility. Joseph used to be proud. He presented his dreams to the family in a spirit of superiority: "you will all bow down to me". However, in his journey through slavery and then prison he learned that he wasn't in control, but God was. Now, as he was standing before Pharaoh, he pulled that lesson from the past into the present. Genesis 41:15-16 "Pharaoh said to Joseph, "I had a dream, and no one can interpret it. But I have heard it said of you that when you hear a dream you can interpret it." "I cannot do it," Joseph replied to Pharaoh, "but God will give Pharaoh the answer he desires."'" He knew that He couldn't, but God could.

- His understanding of the voice of God. Joseph had the ability to hear and understand what God was saying from a young age – he had dreams from heaven that he was able to interpret. One of the great things about Joseph's journey is that the dark times didn't destroy that gift. He could have stood before Pharaoh thinking "look where my gift of dream-interpretation has got me, there's no way I'm using this gift any more"! But he didn't. He dusted it off and started to flow in his prophetic gift, again. Genesis 41:28: Joseph said, "God has shown Pharaoh what he is about to do."

- His skills of stewardship. In Genesis 41:33-36 Joseph explains to Pharaoh how the seven years of good crops should be stewarded so that there is provision in the seven years of drought. Those skills of stewarding were learned in the house of Potiphar. Everything Potiphar had was entrusted to Joseph's care, and it prospered. God helped Joseph learn how to manage the wealth and workforce of another, with excellence. And so, there before Pharaoh, he pulls that skill from his past into the present.

In our past God will have led us through situations that have taught us important lessons. He will have honed the spiritual gifts that He has given to us. He will have put us in situations that have trained us to excel in skills and abilities. If we can pull all that wealth of experience, training and learning into the present then we are in an excellent place to take the next step in our life of glory.

Questions:

- What are the specific skills you have gained so far in your life of glory?
- What specific lessons have you learned so far in your life of glory?
- How do these lessons and skills prepare you for your future?

The clues in our history

One of the big challenges some Christians face in pursuing their unique life of glory is that they don't really know what they should do next. They appreciate that God has led them, taught them and trained them – but what do they do with all that? In the next chapter we will see that God has ways of showing us what our future will look like – the Bible, the prophetic gift, our passions and desires all point us towards what we should do in our next season.

But before we look at that, we need to learn that our history also contains some great clues as to where God is wanting to take us in the future.

Coming back to Joseph, in some ways it is no surprise that he landed the job Pharaoh gave him. His resumé perfectly matched the role. Genesis 41:38-39 "So Pharaoh asked [his officials], "Can we find anyone like this man, one in whom is the spirit of God?" Then Pharaoh said to Joseph, "Since God has made all this known to you, there is no one so discerning and wise as you."" (NIV) He was gifted, anointed and skilled for the position of stewarding the bumper crops in ways that brought provision in the lean years. Joseph could never have planned to become Prime Minister, but by looking at his past he could easily have concluded that God wanted him to flow in prophetic stewardship.

Our past won't reveal the precise nature of our next step, but it can show us the general direction of travel. The experiences, lessons and training that God has brought you through not only prepare you for the next season of glory, they can also help you discern what the next step in that journey should be.

Ask yourself these questions:

- What experiences have I been through? The chances are that God has allowed you to go through experiences that have given you insight into the areas of service that He is calling you into. For example, if you have been through specific life-issues He might be setting you up to minister to people with those same issues. If you have experience of different cultures, then He may have put you on a path to minister cross-culturally.

- What skills have I gained? In your personal life, professional life or church life you will have gained specific skills. Perhaps teaching, caring, practical, financial and so on. God has taken you on a journey where you have been trained in these things. There is every possibility that God has set you on a path where these skills will be used in greater ways to demonstrate His mercy and grace. Equally, consider things you've tried, but haven't been that great at mastering. There is every chance God is leading you away from those areas of work, ministry and service.

- What life-lessons have I learned? There will be times in your past where you have come up against a problem and have overcome. That may be in your relationships, leadership, employment, ministry or other areas of life. God has taught you things in your past which will channel you into your future.

By considering the experiences we have had, the skills we have gained and the lessons we have learned, we can get a 'feel' for where God might be leading us into next.

> **Question:**
>
> - What 'clues' can you see from your own experiences, skills and life-lessons that may point towards the next step in your life of glory?

Above what we imagine

Throughout this chapter, we've seen that thinking about our history is powerful in moving us from glory to glory. As we declare the way that God has kept us, we actually declare His grace and mercy. As we meditate on our past experiences, skills and lessons then, like Joseph, we can get a sense of what our next step might be. We also appreciate that God wants to use the whole of our history to equip us for a future season. But there's something we should always bear in mind as we move from glory to glory: our future is beyond our current understanding.

1 Corinthians 2:9 "However, as it is written: "What no eye has seen, what no ear has heard, and what no human mind has conceived" - the things God has prepared for those who love him." (NIV)

Ephesians 3:20-21 "Now to him who is able to do immeasurably more than all we ask or imagine, according to his power that is at work within us, to him be glory in the church and in Christ Jesus throughout all generations, for ever and ever! Amen." (NIV)

God has prepared for us more than we can currently see; He is able to do more in our lives than we can currently imagine. Therefore, our history does not limit what God will lead us into. Joseph was prepared for the work of Prime Minister through his history, but it would have taken him by surprise when he landed the job! Same with you. Your history is a work of God's glory, through which He has equipped you to take your next steps – but where that will lead is greater than anything you can imagine right now. Your history is a springboard from which God wants you to launch into your next step in the life of unimaginable glory.

Questions:

- Do you feel your past has put limits on you? If so, what could you do to gain a mindset that 'your future is not limited by your past'?
- If you could accomplish anything for the glory of God what would it be?

Looking forward

The next chapter will cover some more details on how you can discover the specific things that God wants you to do in your future life of glory. The chapter after that is all about how living well today can help you to move forward. Then, the final chapter will paint a picture of how your world can be impacted as you pursue the life of glory.

"God, thank you for the way your grace has led me to today. Help me to learn to embrace every aspect of my history to launch into the next step of my life of glory."

Reading the pages of your future

Already written

An important key in moving forward in the life of glory is working out what God is saying about our future. Many Christians understand that God wants great things for them and He wants to use them in great ways to demonstrate His grace and mercy to the world. However, many Christians struggle to discern the specifics of what that means for the next season in their lives. They simply don't know what the pages of their future look like, or what God is calling them to. Discovering where your future should be heading is the purpose of this chapter.

Before diving into discovering what God says about your future understand this: God has already written about your future in His book. Psalm 139:16 "all the days ordained for me were <u>written in your book</u> before one of them came to be." He sees everything that is going to happen to you and He sees everything that you are going to accomplish for Him; and He's already written it down in a book. God wants us to learn to read this book, because through it we can receive clear direction about the specific path that God is calling us to go down in pursuing our life of glory.

Questions:

- How does knowing that God has already written about your future make you feel about what lies ahead in your life?
- Have you ever had direction from God about your next step in life? If so, how did you receive this direction?

An important thing to note about the book of your life, is that each chapter can be very different from the previous. Earlier in this book you saw that we need to leave one stage of glory to move into the next. The steps of glory that God is calling you to in the future may look very different to what He called you to in the past. That's why we need to consider this question many times in our lives. It really isn't a question of discovering what God wants for your life and then sticking to that until your grave. It's about discovering what God is saying about the next season of your life and then stepping into your next phase of glory.

Another important point about the book of your life is: what God has already written about you reflects the choices you will make.

Real life doesn't just unfold, it changes direction in response to our actions and attitudes. It takes twists and turns as we make decisions about our relationships, careers and ministries. God knows exactly what decisions you will make. Therefore, the choices that you make have a big influence on what God has already written about your future. If you choose to pursue the life of glory, then God will have already written chapters about how you are going to demonstrate His grace and mercy in powerful ways. If you choose not to pursue the life of glory, then that book will already contain a very different narrative. Learning to read what He has written about our future will help you to move into those steps.

Questions:

- How easy or difficult is it for you to leave one phase of glory to move into a new season of glory; to step into something completely new in your life of glory? Why?
- In what ways do the decisions that people make in the present affect what God has written about their future?

Works that bring glory

The Bible says in Ephesians 2:10, that "we are God's handiwork, created in Christ Jesus to do good works, which God prepared in advance for us to do." (NIV) There is something powerful about the Greek word for 'works' ('ergon') in that verse – it means 'work'! So, when we talk about taking the next step in the life of glory, we are talking about what God actually wants us to *do* in the next season of our lives.

We see that God has saved us by His grace and mercy and re-created us in Christ Jesus to *do* the work that He has already prepared! Jesus gives us a big clue as to what the nature of those works will be in Matthew 5:16: "In the same way, let your light shine before others, that they may see your good deeds and glorify your Father in heaven." (NIV) Whatever the specific work is that God calls you to, it will be focussed on helping other see His glory. Remember that the glory of God is seen in His grace and mercy. Therefore, we can only begin to discover what God wants for us when we pursue a future that demonstrates mercy and grace.

Question:

- Make a list of the type of work that you can do that will help others see the glory of God.

Uniqueness

God's work of natural creation is infinitely diverse: every snow-drop, every flower, every tree and every person is different. Equally, every work of God's new creation is unique. There are a lot of things in common with every Christian: they are all forgiven, justified, have hope and purpose. But equally, every Christian is unique. God doesn't make clones; He makes individuals. In every believer God has placed different desires, hopes and dreams. He has given different believers different skills and gifts – both natural and spiritual. God has placed things in you that He has not placed in others. He wants to draw these things out of you in increasing measures in a way that causes people to glorify Him. Being comfortable with this uniqueness is an important key in discovering the works of glory that God's has prepared for you to do.

> **Question:**
>
> - In what ways do Christians struggle to appreciate their uniqueness?

In particular, there are three things about your uniqueness that can help you recognise your next step in your journey from glory to glory.

- Desires. Psalm 37:4 "Take delight in the LORD, and he will give you the desires of your heart." This is not about God bringing about everything we want. It's about God showing us the unique desires that He has placed in our heart and then enabling us to step into them. God has put within you a unique passion to do something glorious, and that passion is linked closely to what God is calling you to do. This will be different for every Christian. Some will be focussed on social justice, others on politics, others on education or some form of church leadership. To read the pages of our future we need to 'tune in' to the desire that He has placed in our hearts. We do that by delighting in Him; simply spending time soaking up His presence.

- Gifts. 1 Corinthians 12:4 & 11 "There are different kinds of gifts, but the same Spirit distributes them... All these are the work of one and the same Spirit, and he distributes them to each one, just as he determines." (NIV) 1 Corinthians 12:8-11 lists 9 gifts of the Spirit. Ephesians 4:11 lists 5 gifts of Christ. 1 Corinthians 12:28 lists gifts such as helping and giving guidance. Other gifts mentioned in the Bible are generosity, hospitality and even martyrdom (although you can only give that one once!). Every Christian has a unique gift set given to them by God. It is important to note that God only leads us into areas of service that He equips us for; He will never expect you to do things that He has not gifted you in. Therefore, understanding our unique set of God-given gifts helps us discover what He wants us to do in our future life of glory. (In this book there isn't scope to go through what all these gifts are, but if you learn more about them you will begin to recognise that God has given some of them to you.)

- Connections. Every person in the world has a unique set of connections. Everyone has a different group of friends, family and acquaintances. God usually works in the context of relationships because relationships bring opportunities; we can only demonstrate the grace and mercy of God to others when we have a connection to them. Therefore, who we relate to is a great pointer to what God is calling us to do.

Something interesting about our unique desires, gifts and connections is that they change over the course of our lives. As we grow naturally and spiritually we change. That's why it is good to consider these things at different times in our lives. As already stated in this chapter, we need to be discovering where God is leading us next, and not assume that is in the same way as in the past. Looking carefully at what desires, skills and connections you have at this stage of your life will help you read what God has already written about your next season of glory.

Questions:

- What is the greatest desire that God has placed in you?
- What are your three or four most effective skills; the things you can do the best?
- Who do you connect with the most?
- From the above, what type of 'works' do you think God might have prepared for you in your future?

Reading lights

Because life is a blend of these desires, gifts and connections it can all become a bit intertwined and fuzzy. Through those things we can pick out the shape of what God is saying, but there is often a lack of clarity. It's like trying to read in the dark. You can pick out shapes of letters and perhaps the whole of some words, but it's not clear. What sheds light on the pages of our future, and brings things into focus, is the Word of God: Psalm 119:105 "Your <u>word</u> is a lamp for my feet, a <u>light</u> on my path." (NIV)

God speaks to us in many different ways. Firstly, the Bible is His written Word that helps to bring clarity about what He is calling us to do. As you have seen throughout this book, the Bible is clear about the general nature of a life of glory: it is about doing works that declare and demonstrate the grace and mercy of Jesus to the heavens and the world. God can also use the Bible to bring clarity about the specific things He's calling you to do as you pursue the life of glory. It may be that as you read the Bible, a phrase or idea 'jumps off the page' which God uses to speak more clearly about your future. This is a very important way in which God speaks, and it can be helpful to make notes about what you feel God is saying to you as you read the Bible.

However, there are other ways in which God speaks that can bring clarity to our understanding about the specific works of glory He wants us to do. Two of these are explained here:

- Prophecy. This is where someone else tells you what they believe God wants you to know. Prophecy can be used by God to tell you something about your future or something that will equip and encourage you to step into that future. Both aspects are important, and both can shed light on where God is leading you. For example, you may sense that God is calling you to work with children because of your desire, gifts and connections but don't know where. If someone then prophesies that they see you serving God among African orphans the prophetic word adds light, more clarity to God's word to you. Or perhaps someone might prophesy that God is giving you a greater level of influence at work, which encourages you to take a promotion you weren't sure was right. However, note that people can only 'prophesy in part' (1 Corinthians 13:9). It is important not to take a prophetic word as the complete word from God – it is a part-word.

- Peace. The Bible teaches us that God speaks direct to our spirits. One of the most significant ways He does this is through giving us peace about a certain course of action. Colossians 3:15 says "Let the peace of Christ rule in your hearts." The Greek word for 'rule' is 'brabeuo', which literally means 'arbitrate'. When you are trying to work through the will of God for your next season, the peace of God will arbitrate; it will shed light on whether a course of action is right or wrong. For example, you may sense that God wants you to start a new job to give you more opportunity to demonstrate His glory to the world. By paying attention to whether God is giving you peace about it or not will shed light on whether God wants you to take the job.

Through prophecy and peace God can speak to you. In that, God will shed light on whether you are hearing Him correctly about your next season. That will help us read the pages of our future with increasing clarity.

Questions:

- Have you ever had a prophetic word that has helped you discover the next thing that God is wanting you to do? If so, describe the word and what happened.
- Have you ever thought about doing something, or started doing something, and felt uneasy about it? If so, did you carry on or stop and what was the result?

Keeping on track

As you have seen in this chapter, you can learn to read the pages of your future when you focus on grace and mercy; recognise your unique desires, gifts and connections; and have the light of God's Word. However, because we are always in the 'learning' stage we can never be 100% correct 100% of the time. It is possible for us to get confused and mistaken about what the next step in our life of glory should be. Therefore, God has also given us boundaries that are 100% clear to keep us on the right path whilst we discover His plan for our lives.

In Matthew 7:14 Jesus says, "Small is the gate and <u>narrow</u> the road that leads to <u>life</u>, and only a few find it." (NIV) The life that God wants us to live (the life of glory), is narrow. God has given us the boundaries of a narrow path to keep us safe as we discover what our next step should be. The boundaries of this narrow path are set down in the Bible.

It is not unknown for Christians to have desires that go against what God has said in His written Word. They have even heard prophetic words that could be interpreted to confirm their desires. In response they have stepped into a future that takes them further away from where God wants them to be. This principle is absolutely essential in pursuing a life of glory: The book of our life must always fall in line with the book of God, the Bible. No matter what your desires, skills and connections are. No matter what prophetic Words you get or what peace you experience. The life of glory never takes us down a path that causes us to go against what God has said in the Bible.

This is the narrow way; a way of pulling our life in line with the principles of scripture. Keep to that path and you will stay safe from the stray feelings, thoughts and desires that sometimes invade your heart and head.

> **Question:**
>
> - What Bible verses do you know that can help you stay on the 'narrow path' as you discover the next works of glory that God is calling you to?

Confidence in God

God says in Isaiah 14:24 "Surely, as I have thought, so it shall come to pass, and as I have purposed, so it shall stand." What God has written about your future is certain. It is a future filled with good works for you to do that enable others to glorify Him. It is a future that is specifically designed around your desires, gifts and connections. By considering our uniqueness and having the light of God's Word we can learn to read what God is saying about our future. That is powerful. You are not a fortune-teller, but you can be a future-discoverer!

However, it is one thing to read the pages of your future, it is another to have the confidence to step into them. At the end of this chapter, know that what God has already written about you will happen. There are no plans too big or bold for God. He's more than able to equip you for the works of glory that He's calling you to. He's more than able to open doors of opportunity for you.

Therefore, don't be content to just know about your path to a life of glory; have the courage to chase after it. Be confident that God will lead you into your next season of effectiveness as you pursue the life of glory.

Looking forward

In the next chapter you will discover that taking all the lessons and experience of the past, and putting it into great use in the present, enables you to step into the future works of glory that God has prepared for you. The final chapter of this book then describes how our world can be radically changed if we all pursue this life.

"God help me to know the next step in my life of glory and recognise the works that you want me to do that will enable others to bring glory to you. Then, give me courage to step into my future with confidence in you."

Living in the now

Glory in you

Throughout this book you have seen that God has given you a life of glory to grow in. When you came to faith, you entered in to that way of living. God then has works which He has prepared for you to do, that will enable others to glorify the Father. You have seen that this plan of God for your life will always be outworked in the context of His wider purposes for the world and the Church; and we can discover what those works are as we learn to read the pages of our future. A great springboard into our next season is available for us, if we can pull all our experience from the past into the present.

However, in this journey from glory to glory there is a very real danger: it is possible to become so focussed on what we will enter into, that we don't appreciate the glory that we have in the present. It is, therefore, important to remember that pursuing a life of glory is not just about looking forward to the amazing things God will do through us; it is also about living in the glory every day.

As stated in the previous chapter, you already have a measure of glory in you even though there may be things in your life that seem inglorious. That glory, fundamentally, is our life in Jesus. Colossians

1:27 tells us that Christ <u>in us</u> is the 'hope of glory'. The Greek word for 'hope' there is 'elpis', which means 'expectation' or 'confidence'. From that, we see our Christian hope is not 'wishing for something' but having confidence that it is ours, even if we can't yet see it. Whatever is going on in your life today, if you have Christ in you, then you can be confident that the glory of God is residing in you. The psalmist expresses this confidence when he writes "the boundary lines have fallen for me in pleasant places; surely I have a delightful inheritance." (Psalm 16:6, NIV). If you have Jesus, right now, the boundaries of your life have fallen in good places.

Questions:

- In what ways can focussing solely on the future blind us to what God is wanting to do in our lives today?
- Regardless of whatever else is happening in your life right now, how does having Jesus in your life help give you an experience of the glory of God?

Destined for the present, as well as future

In this season of your life, God has not only put glory in you, He also wants to show His glory through you. Esther's uncle, Mordecai recognised this when he said to her "Yet who knows whether you have come to the kingdom for <u>such a time as this</u>?" (Esther 4:14, NIV) Esther was cut off from the support of her family, she was under threat from the enemies of the Jews and her husband had not wanted to see her for a month. Her life was far from great. Yet, right there, God had an amazing work for her to do which would bring glory to Him.

Like Esther, where you are now can be as much a place of destiny as your future. In your life of glory, you've stepped from your past and you are walking towards your next season. That means that you are currently living in the middle of the journey; you are in the centre of a glorious life. Out of everything you learn in this chapter, remember this key thought: the life of glory isn't just our future destiny, it's our current reality.

Proverbs 3:5-6 "Trust in the LORD with all your heart, And lean not on your own understanding; In all your ways acknowledge Him, And He shall <u>direct your path</u>." (NKJV) Let's pull that verse from the future and into a present context. Most Christians do their best at trusting in God; they try their hardest to follow His plans. You may have made mistakes in the journey, but generally you will have done your best to stay on course. If you have done that, then God has directed your paths. And it follows that if God has directed your paths, He has directed you to the place you find yourself today. You may not like it, or you may really like it. It might be a day of fruitfulness or barrenness. You may not understand how God could have led you to the place you are in. But if you have committed your ways to God, you now find yourself in the place where He wants you to be.

That sounds great when everything feels blessed. It provokes a serious question if things are bad: Is my situation really God's will for my life? Has God really destined me for this? The answer is yes and no. No, because God has more glory for you to step into. Yes, because it is part of the journey.

Right now, wherever you are, you are just at one point in your life of glory. God has directed your steps to the place where you find yourself today. He's not taken you off course. And, from this place He will lead you on. Remember that in Psalm 23 the journey is by still waters and through the valley of the shadow of death; finally, there is the banquet.

Recognising that God has works of glory for us to do in our current circumstances is important for two reasons:

- God wants you to be successful in the opportunities He has given you for now. Looking towards your future is great, but not at the expense of missing God's plan for your today.

- How we respond to our present situation will either trap us or release us into our next season of glory. Living well now enables us to move on. Bad attitudes hold us back.

The rest of this chapter contains some thoughts that will help you to make the most of your present life of glory in a way that will help you move on to the next step.

Questions:

- How do you feel about the statement "the life of glory isn't just our future destiny, it's our current reality"?
- Do you believe that God has led you to where you are today? Why or why not?

Confidence in the presence

Psalm 23:6 "Even though I walk through the darkest valley, I will fear no evil, for you are with me; your rod and your staff, they comfort me." (NIV) Note that God doesn't say that He is going to heal or do the miraculous. God is simply going to be present in the valley.

It is possible to focus so much on what we want God to do in our situation that we forget who He *is* in our situation. For example, someone who is sick may feel that the only way they can experience and demonstrate the glory of God is through being healed. So, their whole life becomes focussed on that – they become completely absorbed with what they want God to do. But understand this: God can use a sick or disabled person as much as someone who is physically well or able-bodied. Sickness or disability does not affect the level of glory; it doesn't affect God's ability to use someone to demonstrate His grace and mercy. His presence is all you need to be able show His glory to the world, despite the valley you are going through.

You should continue to look for God's power to impact your life and others. He wants to bring deliverance, restoration and healing. But it is equally important not to lose sight of His presence. Regardless of what God does in your situation, He is always the God who is with us. And that presence is all we need to experience and demonstrate His glory to the world, today.

Question:

- Have you ever been in a situation where God has not done what you wanted Him to do, but you still sensed His presence? What happened and what came out of that season?
- What can you do, practically, to keep a strong focus on the presence of God when you don't see His power at work in your circumstances?

Recognise the opportunity of now

Sometimes people feel that their current circumstances prevent them from doing the works of glory that God has prepared for them. The reality of life is that there will be times when you are restricted; you simply won't have the opportunity to do everything you believe God wants you to do. That can be because of your work, family, or other things. And, can bring great frustration. You ask God: why don't I have the opportunity to do what you have called me to?

A very important lesson to note here is this: the only real opportunity you have to demonstrate God's grace and mercy is now. You will get more in the future, but now is the place that God has brought you to. Now is the chance you have to flow in the works of glory that God has prepared for this season. If you can embrace that, instead of just waiting for the new and greater opportunities to open up, then something dynamic happens. You start to fulfil the call of God on your life in the present.

Another important lesson is that taking the now-opportunities to demonstrate the glory of God opens the door to the next opportunities. David is a great example. In the dark valley of war, he took the opportunity to kill a giant. That opened the door to King Saul's palace. In the palace, David took the opportunity to soothe Saul when he was tormented by an evil spirit. That opened the door to becoming a commander in the army. As a commander, David took the opportunity to lead his men well. That opened the door to kingship. Making the most of the opportunities God gives us in the present phase of our life of glory opens doors to the next.

Right now, you may feel restricted in your journey from glory to glory but learn to embrace the moment. Your current opportunities to demonstrate God's mercy and grace is not your final destiny. But, they are part of your journey.

Questions:

- What are the current opportunities you have to use your unique skills and connections in ways that enable other people to bring glory to God?
- Do you have any personal examples of how making the most of your current opportunities opens the door to new opportunities?
- What advice would you give to someone who felt very restricted in their job or ministry?

Learn the lessons of now

In the same way that our past contains lessons that we can pull into the present, our current circumstances can teach us important things that equip us for our future. If we learn well, in the now, we are better enabled to pursue the life of glory in our future.

Usually we learn more through the difficult times than the good. Struggles, problems and temptations shape us and change us into the image of Christ more than the blessings.

The Bible clearly shows us that God does not cause bad things to happen to 'teach us a lesson': James 1:13 says "When tempted, no one should say, "God is tempting me." For God cannot be tempted by evil, <u>nor does he tempt anyone</u>." (NIV) But it also teaches us that the life of glory will take us through some very difficult situations. Romans 8:17 tells us that "we share in his sufferings in order that we may also share in his glory." (NIV) There are times when God may redirect your path to avoid trouble, but a lot of the time He won't. He doesn't cause suffering but if it's in the way of you getting to the next season of glory He will lead you through it. Sometimes, we have to walk through the valley, so we can get to the banquet (see Psalm 23). In this way, a valley can be the place the God has led you to. Just as the Spirit led Jesus into the wilderness, and ultimately God led Him to the cross, so God will lead us through times of suffering. The cross wasn't the final destination, but it was a step along the way to glory.

In your valley God wants you to learn. That might be a lesson of commitment, obedience or something else. If you are currently going through a valley experience then learn to embrace it; allow it to shape you, then you will be better equipped to take another step in the life of glory.

Questions:

- How do you feel about the statement that if trouble is 'in the way of you getting to the next season of glory God will lead you through it.'?
- What have you learned about yourself, others and God in times of trouble? How have those lessons helped you?

Contentment with vision

God has brought you to this place in your life of glory. If you have tried to live for Him, then you are on the right path. He's not taken you off course. This is a point along your path. It's not the end, but it is where God has brought you to for this moment. Embrace today as a step in the journey from glory to glory. In your present circumstances know the presence, use your current opportunities, learn from the Spirit. Don't just wait for the future, because you will only get to the next step in God when you have embraced this one.

Finally, be content with now. Don't stop looking for the next step but relax into this season of glory. 1 Timothy 6:6 says that "godliness with <u>contentment</u> is great gain." (NIV) In other words, being satisfied with what God is doing now, coupled with a vision of God's glory is hugely powerful. Some people think that contentment is the enemy of vision; if we are content with now, we won't want to move on to the next thing. But if we compliment vision with contentment we are more empowered to move on in God. Why? Because when we are in the place of being satisfied with God we are saturated by His presence, serve with confidence and grow in character. All that prepares you for the next step. From a place of being content in every situation and embracing it as part of your journey, you are better placed to pursue more of the life of glory.

Looking forward

So far in this book you have seen how God has a great life of glory for you that He wants to out-work in the context of His eternal purpose; Through gazing on the grace and mercy of Jesus you can being to move forward in this journey; If we can pull all the experience of the past into the present we have a great springboard into our next season; We can discover what God is calling us to as we learn to read the pages of our future; And to take that next step, we need to be embracing the current season.

In the final chapter of this book you will be presented with a vision of what the world would be like if every Christian pursued this life of glory.

"God, help me to embrace the place that you have led me to for now. I choose to make the most of my current opportunities to demonstrate your glory to my world."

Living in the now: Journal

Heaven on earth

God's answer to prayer

In Matthew 6:10, Jesus prayed "your kingdom come, your will be done, on earth as it is in heaven." He was asking for the glory of heaven to be known on earth. That echo's what was mentioned in chapter one of this book: God wants His glory to be known as the waters cover the sea. As stated in that chapter, God's purpose for the Church is to narrow the gap between the reality that God's glory covers the earth and the experience of people who are often oblivious to that glory.

Therefore, the answer to Jesus' prayer, which has been repeated by every generation of Christian, is actually us. The Church is the vehicle by which God's Kingdom is known in the earth and the means by which His will is fulfilled. As you saw at the beginning of this book, there will come a time when God's glory illuminates a new heaven and earth. But, in this current period of eternity, God has chosen the Church, which is full of imperfect people to bring a revelation of His perfect mercy and grace to the world.

As you also saw in chapter one, God's purpose for the Church will only be outworked as every individual Christian takes their place in

His plan. This whole book has been about how we understand what that personal plan is for our lives and how we can take the next step in being transformed from glory to glory. This means that you, as an individual, are part of the answer to Jesus' prayer 'let your kingdom come'.

> **Question:**
>
> - How do you feel about the phrase that you "are part of the answer to Jesus' prayer 'let your kingdom come'"?

Obviously, as an individual you cannot bring the whole of heaven to all the world. But, you can bring something of heaven to your sphere of influence on earth. The people who you relate to can, and should, experience something of the power and glory of heaven through you. That's what the life of glory accomplishes.

So, as you live in the life of glory, you bring a bit of heaven to your bit of earth. If every Christian did that, just imagine what the impact would be. "The earth [would] be <u>filled</u> with the knowledge of the glory of the LORD, as the waters cover the sea." (Habakkuk 2:14, NIV) As an individual, you have the potential to fill your world with the knowledge of the glory of the Lord. Together, we have the potential to fill the whole earth with the knowledge of the glory of the Lord.

Again, as an individual, and as the Church, we are the answer to Jesus's prayer: let your kingdom come.

Questions:

- In what ways can the church, as a whole, increase the knowledge of the glory of God in all the earth?
- Think back to the previous chapter, where you considered the people you relate to. In what practical ways are you able to bring a bit of heaven into their lives?

What heaven on earth looks like

An interesting question to consider is this: what would things look like if I brought a knowledge of heaven into my world? Isaiah 61 gives us as few pointers in answering that question. It tells us that when we live as God has called us to live, then certain things happen on earth.

- Good news is proclaimed to the poor (Isaiah 61:1). In your world there will be people who live in poverty – financially, spiritually and emotionally. What poor people need more than anything else is news of hope. They don't necessarily need people to sort their problems out for them; they need to be empowered to move from poverty to prosperity. This is the message of the gospel. And, as we demonstrate the good news of God's salvation then the poor have the hope of richness through Jesus.

- Broken-hearted people are healed (Isaiah 61:2a). There will be people you come across who are broken (every one of us is broken at some level). That gives us an opportunity to bring healing. As you saw in chapter two, living in the glory of God enables us to release His power into people's lives. Sick people become healthy. Hurting relationships are soothed. Mourning gives way to joy. Whilst there will always be a level of brokenness in your world, releasing the glory of heaven makes it much more scarce.

- Captives are freed (Isaiah 61:2b). Some people in your world will find themselves 'in a box'. They are restricted by their circumstances, behaviours or thought-patterns. But we have confidence that God renews minds, gives ability to change actions and lifts people out of negative situations. In demonstrating the grace and mercy of Jesus, we provide people with a means of escape from their personal prisons.

- Favour is released (Isaiah 61:2). God is generous. He's given us all things (Romans 8:32). And out of the favour we have received, we give. As we share provision, skills and gifts that God has given to us then others benefit. They experience an overflow of God's favour from our lives. In response they can begin to look for and receive that favour for themselves.

- Grief, mourning and despair turn to joy (Isaiah 61:2-3). When we bring heaven to our world then the atmosphere changes from desperation to joyfulness. Your very presence can dispel depressive and oppressive moods. When you bring heaven into a room there comes a lightness. Burdens are lifted, and heaviness is off-loaded.

These are the heavenly things that Jesus brought to earth. And by living in the glory of Christ we can ooze an atmosphere of heaven into our world in the same way.

> **Questions:**
>
> - Where are the opportunities for you to bring an 'atmosphere of heaven'?
> - How can you demonstrate the glory of heaven to people you know, particularly thinking about the things seen in Isaiah 61 (hope, healing, freedom, favour and joy)?
> - Think about some people you know. How would their lives look if they experienced hope, healing, freedom, favour and joy?

Anointed with the Spirit of glory

Isaiah 61 starts with the words "The Spirit of the Sovereign LORD is on me, because the LORD has <u>anointed</u> me..." (NIV) 2 Corinthians 3:18 tells us that our transformation from glory to glory comes from "the Lord, who is the Spirit" (NIV). Peter describes the Holy Spirit as the '<u>Spirit of glory</u>' (1 Peter 4:4).

We can see from those Bible verses that the anointing to bring heaven to earth is from the person of the Holy Spirit. Simply, the life of glory is one that is anointed by the Spirit of glory. And, through this anointing we see an increase in the knowledge of God's glory in our world.

Every real Christian will have a passion to bring something of heaven to earth; to be part of the answer to Jesus' prayer "let your kingdom come". You should be stirred as you imagine the difference your life of glory will make in the world. Through this book you have seen some important lessons on how to do that:

- Recognise your place in God's purpose for the church;
- Gain momentum as you grow in glory;
- Pull the experiences of your past into the present;
- Learn to read the pages of your future; and
- Live in the now.

All those things will help you discover and take the next step in your life of glory. However, above all that, you will only be able to bring heaven to earth through the anointing of the Holy Spirit. It is through Him that the power and glory of heaven is given to you and then flows through you. If you really want to be part of seeing the knowledge of the glory of God increase in your world then you need have an increase of anointing by the Spirit of glory.

Receiving that anointing requires a mind-set of demonstration, not protection. Very often, Christians will talk about how being full of the Holy Spirit has an amazing impact on their lives. It does. And sometimes Christians will seek to keep that to themselves. But the Spirit of glory doesn't anoint us to keep the glory; He anoints us to demonstrate it to the world. If we have a mind-set is focussed on demonstrating the glory of God in increasing measures, then the Spirit of glory anoints us in increasing measure. And the more we are anointed the more we can bring good news to the poor, healing to the broken and freedom to the captives.

Questions:

- What do you think are the differences between a mind-set of demonstration and protection?
- What impact has the Holy Spirit made on your life?
- How do you think you can receive more of the anointing of the Holy Spirit?

As this book comes to a close, be encouraged to pursue this life of glory. Put into action everything you have learned. But, above all that, pursue the Spirit of glory. It is He who will lead you step by step as you journey from glory to glory and bring the glory of heaven to your world.

"God, I ask that you anoint me with the Spirit of glory so that I will be transformed more into your glory and bring something of heaven to my world."

Printed in Poland
by Amazon Fulfillment
Poland Sp. z o.o., Wrocław